Withdrawn

D0943826

CHLOE KIM

BY DEREK MOON

SportsZone

An Imprint of Abdo Publishing
abdopublishing.com

abdopublishing.com

Published by Abdo Publishing, a division of ABDO, PO Box 398166, Minneapolis, Minnesota 55439. Copyright © 2019 by Abdo Consulting Group, Inc. International copyrights reserved in all countries. No part of this book may be reproduced in any form without written permission from the publisher. SportsZone™ is a trademark and logo of Abdo Publishing.

Printed in the United States of America, North Mankato, Minnesota
042018
012018

THIS BOOK CONTAINS
RECYCLED MATERIALS

Cover Photo: Mike Egerton/Press Association/PA Wire URN:34923915/AP Images
Interior Photos: Tom Pennington/Getty Images Sport/Getty Images, 4-5, 6, 7, 8-9; Angel La Canfora/Shutterstock Images, 10-11; Shutterstock Images, 12-13; RJ Sangosti/The Denver Post/Getty Images, 14-15; Julie Jacobson/AP Images, 16; Nathan Bilow/Agence Zoom/Getty Images Sport/Getty Images, 17; ImageSpace/Sipa USA/AP Images, 18; Sean M. Haffey/Getty Images Sport/Getty Images, 19, 20-21; Anna Stonehouse/The Aspen Times/AP Images, 22; Gregory Bull/AP Images, 23, 24-25, 28; Lee Jin-man/AP Images, 26-27; Tetsu Joko/The Yomiuri Shimbun/AP Images, 29

Editor: Patrick Donnelly
Series Designer: Jake Nordby

Library of Congress Control Number: 2018936262

Publisher's Cataloging-in-Publication Data

Names: Moon, Derek, author.
Title: Chloe Kim / by Derek Moon.
Description: Minneapolis, Minnesota : Abdo Publishing, 2019. | Series: Olympic Stars Set 2
  | Includes online resources and index.
Identifiers: ISBN 9781532116070 (lib.bdg.) | ISBN 9781532157059 (ebook)
Subjects: LCSH: Kim, Chloe, 2000---Juvenile literature. | Olympic athletes--Juvenile
  literature. | Winter Olympics--Juvenile literature. | Women snowboarders--Juvenile
  literature. | Women medalists--Juvenile literature.
Classification: DDC 796.93092 [B]--dc23

CONTENTS

UNBELIEVABLE 4

CALIFORNIA GIRL 10

TEEN SENSATION 14

OLYMPIC CHAMPION 20

TIMELINE 30
GLOSSARY 31
INDEX 32
ABOUT THE AUTHOR 32

Chloe Kim wows the crowd at the 2016
US Snowboarding Grand Prix.

UNBELIEVABLE

Chloe Kim could have been bitter. She was
one of the best snowboarders in the world.
In fact, she had qualified for the 2014 Olympic
Games. But Olympic rules said snowboarders had
to be 15 years old to compete. Chloe was only
13. She would have to wait.

Instead of being frustrated, Chloe set out to
get better. And in February 2016, she found
herself atop the halfpipe in Park City, Utah.

Under blue skies, Chloe dropped in. She had already won her event at the US Snowboarding Grand Prix. Now it was time to show off.

Showing no fear, Chloe flew up the steep, icy wall. She soared into the air, higher than all of her opponents. The big trick was next. For her second hit, Chloe grabbed her board and spun all the way around. Then she spun again, and once more. In all, she spun 1,080 degrees—three full circles.

Chloe grabs her board to execute a tricky spin.

Even before her run was over, Chloe knew she had nailed it.

Chloe is all smiles as she celebrates with her mentor, Kelly Clark.

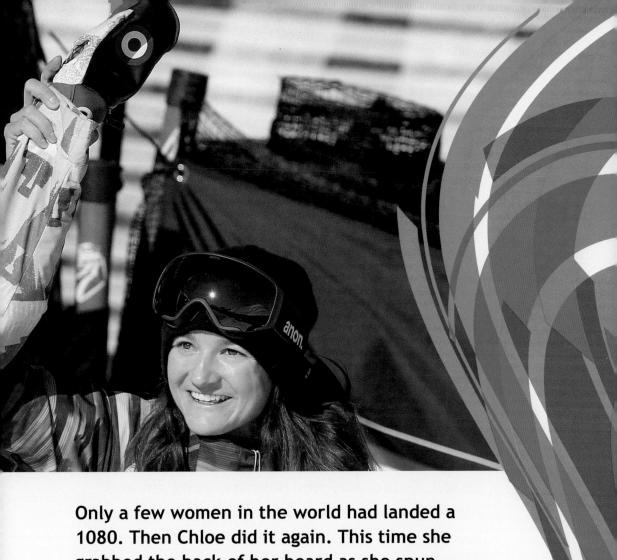

Only a few women in the world had landed a
1080. Then Chloe did it again. This time she
grabbed the back of her board as she spun.
No woman had ever landed back-to-back 1080s.
But no woman was quite like Chloe.

    At the bottom, Chloe couldn't help but smile.
And when her score showed up, her smile grew
even bigger. Chloe had scored a perfect 100.
No woman had done that, either. And at age 15,
Chloe was just getting started.

CALIFORNIA GIRL

Chloe Kim was born on April 23, 2000, in Long Beach, California. Her parents, Jong Jin and Boran Yun, were born in South Korea. They had moved to California before Chloe was born. Their Korean heritage played a big role in Chloe's childhood. But she was a California kid.

Southern California was the perfect spot for Chloe. She grew up in Torrance and enjoyed living near the beach. But at age 4 she started to spend a lot more time around snow. That's when Jong Jin took her to a local resort to try snowboarding.

Chloe spent plenty of time at the beach growing up in Torrance, California.

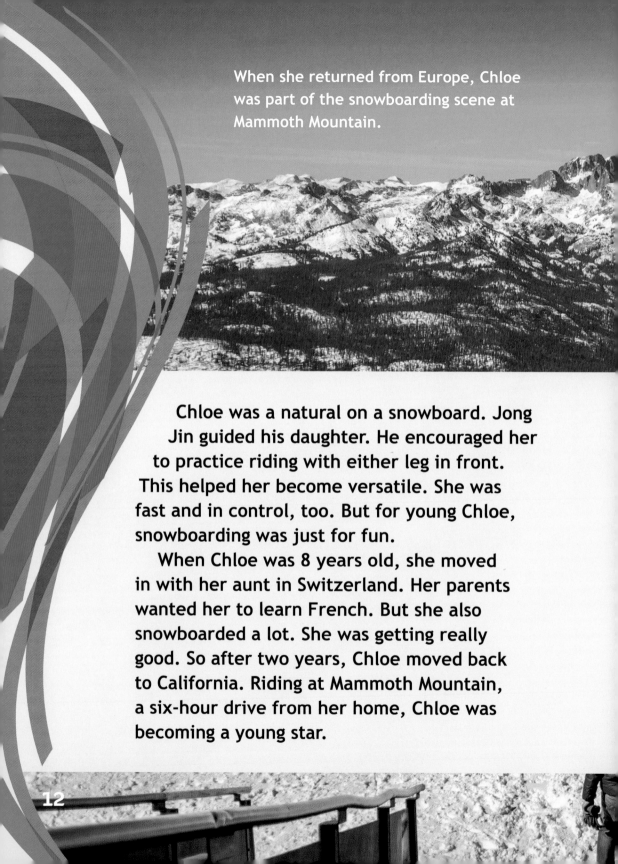

When she returned from Europe, Chloe was part of the snowboarding scene at Mammoth Mountain.

Chloe was a natural on a snowboard. Jong Jin guided his daughter. He encouraged her to practice riding with either leg in front. This helped her become versatile. She was fast and in control, too. But for young Chloe, snowboarding was just for fun.

When Chloe was 8 years old, she moved in with her aunt in Switzerland. Her parents wanted her to learn French. But she also snowboarded a lot. She was getting really good. So after two years, Chloe moved back to California. Riding at Mammoth Mountain, a six-hour drive from her home, Chloe was becoming a young star.

FAST FACT

Chloe began taking online classes while in middle school. This helped her keep up in school despite all of her training and traveling.

TEEN SENSATION

People began to notice Chloe. When she was 11, she got her first sponsor. A snowboarding company paid her to use its equipment. Two years later, she competed at her first X Games. Even with a national TV audience watching, Chloe wasn't fazed. She already rode faster and jumped higher than most women. Chloe's run included a frontside 900. That is two-and-a-half spins. At just 13 years old, she finished second. But when the other riders left for the 2014 Olympics, Chloe had to stay home.

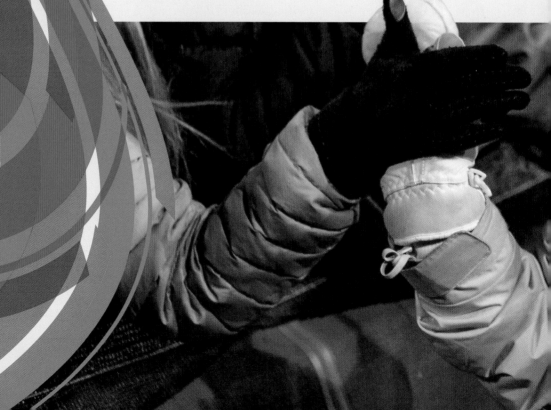

Chloe high fives a fan after finishing second at her first X Games.

By the time she was 13 years old Chloe had begun competing internationally against adults.

FAST FACT

Chloe missed out on the 2014 Olympics. But she got to compete at the 2016 Winter Youth Olympic Games in Norway. Chloe won gold medals in both halfpipe and slopestyle.

Missing the Olympics was tough. Some people thought Chloe could have won a medal. Instead, she used the experience as motivation. When the next season started, Chloe was even better. She won her first X Games title in January 2015. At 14, she was the youngest winner ever. And the next year, Chloe improved even more. She won at both the American and European X Games. She also scored her perfect 100. If ever there was any doubt, now it was clear: Chloe was one of the best in the world.

Chloe stands above Kelly Clark, *left*, and Torah Bright after winning her first X Games title in 2015.

FAST FACT
Growing up in California, Chloe also liked to skateboard. She said skateboarding helped her learn snowboard tricks.

Chloe arrives at Nickelodeon's Kids' Choice Sports 2016.

Everything was going great for Chloe. Companies were lining up to sponsor her. Fans loved her fun, carefree personality. And, most importantly, she was winning. But with the attention came new challenges.

In 2017 Chloe finished third at the X Games. That broke a seven-event winning streak. She struggled in other competitions, too. And at the Olympic test event in South Korea, Chloe got sick. She ended up in the emergency room. The busy schedule had caught up with her. But Chloe finished the season strong. Then she turned her sights to the Olympic year.

Chloe was back in form as the Olympics drew near.

OLYMPIC CHAMPION

Chloe was nervous when she woke up on December 9, 2017. Big competitions were nothing new. But this one was different. Chloe and the other top US snowboarders were in Copper Mountain, Colorado, for the first US Olympic qualifying event. She relaxed when she dropped into the halfpipe. "I think the halfpipe kind of makes me feel at home and all the nerves go away," she said.

It showed. Chloe landed a 1080 on her first run. With a score of 93.75, she moved into first place. Everybody had two more runs to try to catch her. Yet nobody could match Chloe's first run. Then, one week later, Chloe won again. Just like that, she was going to the Olympics.

Nobody could catch Chloe after her first halfpipe run of the day on December 9, 2017.

The X Games were a few days before the Olympics. Competing at night under the lights, Chloe landed back-to-back 1080s. That helped give her a fourth X Games win. She was ready for the Olympics.

The Olympics were in PyeongChang, South Korea. That was a big deal for Chloe. Her parents had grown up in that country. Many relatives still lived there. Everyone was eager to see the teenage star on the Olympic stage. And she did not disappoint. In her Olympic debut, Chloe posted the two highest scores of the day. She was ready for the finals.

Chloe gets big air at the X Games, her final tune-up before the Olympics.

Chloe came on strong during halfpipe qualifying in PyeongChang.

FAST FACT
Chloe is fluent in three languages. She speaks English, French, and Korean.

By the finals, everyone was talking about Chloe. They had watched her high-flying performance the day before. Fans loved her personality. Chloe laughed and smiled between runs. Everyone knew she was having fun. And why wouldn't she?

Like the first round, the finals were in the morning. Also as before, Chloe took the lead on her first run. Other riders tried every trick they could to catch her. It was hopeless. When Chloe came up for her third run, she had already won. It was time for a victory lap.

Chloe reacts as she sees her score after her first run in the finals.

PyeongChang 2018™

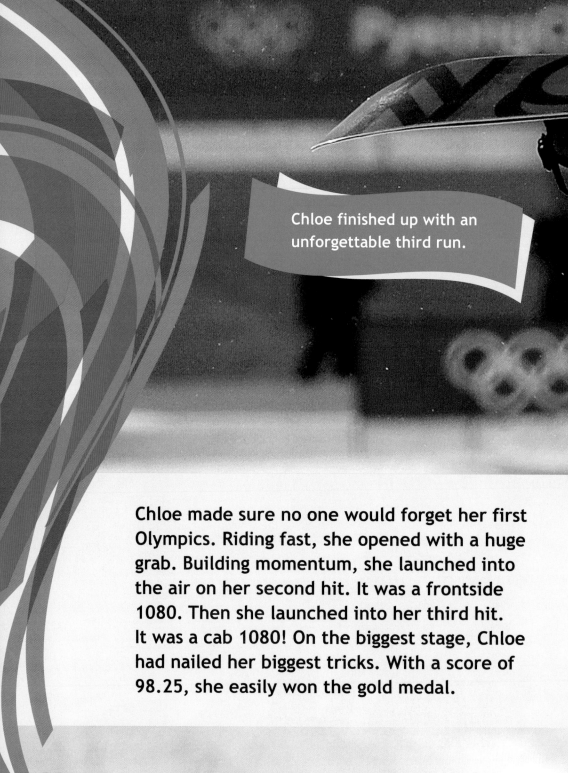

Chloe finished up with an unforgettable third run.

Chloe made sure no one would forget her first Olympics. Riding fast, she opened with a huge grab. Building momentum, she launched into the air on her second hit. It was a frontside 1080. Then she launched into her third hit. It was a cab 1080! On the biggest stage, Chloe had nailed her biggest tricks. With a score of 98.25, she easily won the gold medal.

Ten family members were on hand to watch her winning run. Millions of fans tuned in to the TV broadcasts. They had heard about Chloe's big jumps and stylish tricks. With everything on the line, she delivered a gold-medal performance.

Chloe grabbed an American flag. With her signature wavy hair flowing out from her helmet, she smiled. The Olympics were certainly worth waiting for, she said later. And she was only just getting started.

Chloe proudly sported an American flag as she celebrated her victory.

Four years after having to stay home, Chloe was an Olympic champion.

TIMELINE

2000
Chloe Kim is born on April 23 in Long Beach, California.

2004
When Chloe is 4 years old, her dad, Jong Jin, takes her to a local resort where they learn to snowboard.

2008
Chloe moves to Switzerland, where she lives with her aunt and practices snowboarding for two years.

2010
Chloe returns home to California and begins training at Mammoth Mountain.

2014
At age 13, Chloe becomes the youngest X Games medalist when she wins a silver medal.

2015
Chloe wins her first X Games gold medal. At age 14 she is the youngest X Games gold medal winner.

2016
Chloe wins both halfpipe and slopestyle at the Winter Youth Olympic Games. She turns all her focus to halfpipe soon after.

2016
Chloe makes history by landing back-to-back 1080s and scoring 100 at the US Open in Park City, Utah.

2018
Chloe scores 98.25 on her final run to win the halfpipe gold medal at the Olympics in PyeongChang, South Korea.

GLOSSARY

cab
When a snowboarder spins in the body's natural direction while riding switch, or with her weaker foot forward.

fluent
Able to speak or write a language.

frontside
When a snowboarder spins in the direction of his or her leading shoulder.

halfpipe
An event in which snowboarders are judged for their tricks while riding down a long, U-shaped course.

heritage
The traditions, practices, or beliefs shared by a group that were passed on by their predecessors.

hit
An aerial trick off the top of a halfpipe.

slopestyle
An event in which snowboarders are judged for their tricks off rails, jumps, and other elements.

sponsor
A company that pays an athlete to use and promote its products.

test event
A competition in which athletes try out a facility before it's used for a big event, such as the Olympics.

versatile
Able to adapt to different situations.

victory lap
A run in which a snowboarder has already locked up the win, so she can attempt any tricks she wants.

INDEX

Bright, Torah, 17

Clark, Kelly, 8, 17
Copper Mountain,
   Colorado, 20

Kim, Boran Yun, 10
Kim, Jong Jin, 10, 12

Long Beach,
   California, 10

Mammoth Mountain,
   12

Olympic Games, 5, 14,
   16, 17, 19, 20, 22-29

Park City, Utah, 5-6
PyeongChang, South
   Korea, 22

South Korea, 10, 19,
   22
Switzerland, 12

Torrance, California,
   10

US Snowboarding
   Grand Prix, 6

Winter Youth Olympic
   Games, 16

X Games, 14, 17, 19,
   22

About the Author

Derek Moon is an author and dedicated Stratego player from Watertown, Massachusetts. He dedicates this book to the Fowler family.